THE SOCIETY OF HIGH CONSTABLES

OF

THE CITY OF PERTH

A HISTORY

Researched and compiled by
Mr. J. E. Macmillan, F.S.A. Scot

Edited by
Ex-Moderator C. Roger P. Ward

Published by
The Society of High Constables
of the City of Perth
1992

ISBN 0 9520578 0 8

Printed in Scotland by
Woods of Perth (Printers) Ltd
3–5 Mill Street, Perth, PH1 5JB

PREFACE

by

PROVOST JEAN E.W.McCORMACK, J.P.

As the first lady to become Provost of Perth and Kinross District I am delighted to join with my predecessor, Ex-Provost Alex. Murray, J.P., in commending this History of the Society of High Constables of the City of Perth to all who are interested in Perth heritage. Throughout my ten years' service as a District Councillor I have felt privileged to be associated with such an august body of men - nay gentlemen. It is my intention to further strengthen the bonds between the District Council, the Society of High Constables and the wider community throughout my term of office, and to bask in the protection of one hundred good men and true.

PROVOST JEAN E.W.McCORMACK, J.P.

PREFACE

by

EX-PROVOST ALEX. MURRAY, J.P.

When the honour of Provost was bestowed on me by the District Council in May, 1988, I also discovered that this included an honourable company of men, known as the Society of High Constables of the City of Perth, as my bodyguard. I lost no time in getting in touch with the then Moderator, Mr.James A.McCowan. As a result of this meeting I discovered that for many years the High Constables had hidden their light under a bushel. I am now delighted that the bushel has been removed. I am convinced that the role of the High Constables must be maintained. They are, and always will be, part of Perth past, present and future.

May I take this opportunity to thank all the High Constables for their unfailing support during my term as Provost. Personal thanks to the Ex-Moderator, Mr.Roger Ward, who was of great help in setting up the St.Andrew's Day Youth Service.

I am sure that this publication will be read by people all over the world.

EX-PROVOST ALEX. MURRAY, J.P.

ACKNOWLEDGMENTS

It was in March 1986 that Council first approved the publication of this history and there are many who have given freely of their time and their expertise, to all of whom the Council is greatly indebted, but particularly Perth and Kinross District Council whose support in so many ways has been invaluable.

Eddie Macmillan, local historian and friend of the Society, compiled the historical background, researched extracts from the Minute Books and spent many long hours, with the help of his wife, preparing and typing the original manuscripts from which much of this history has been prepared; we are grateful to them both. Our own sub-committee who read the proofs and contributed valuable advice included Moderator Donald P. McDonald, Ex-Moderator James A. McCowan, Ex-Secretary Michael S. M. Thomson and Ex-Custodiers Graham Fulton and James S. M. Craig. Assistance in tracing suitable illustrations was provided most willingly by the staff of Perth Museum and Art Gallery, particularly Robin Rogers and Paul Adair, and by the Sandeman Library, particularly Stephen Connolly. The Perthshire Advertiser, the Dundee Courier and Louis Flood have kindly provided both photographs and advice, and last, but by no means least, our thanks are due to the Editor, Ex-Moderator Roger Ward.

To all those who have helped, whether they are mentioned by name or not, the Council wishes to express its sincere thanks.

CONTENTS

Society of High Constables.

DRILL.

The Moderator requests the Members of the Society to meet in the City Hall for drill on Monday Evening, the 6th inst., at 8.30 prompt.

You are requested to bring your **Large** and Small Batons.

James Stirton,
Hon. Secretary.

7 High Street,
Perth, 1st April, 1891.

A Drill Notice of 1891

CHAPTER ONE

THE HISTORIC BACKGROUND

The name 'Constable' derives from the Latin 'Comes-Stabuli' - the Count of the Stables of the Roman Emperors - the cavalry of Imperial Rome!

By way of France the Normans introduced the title into England. With the reigns of the sons of Malcolm Canmore and Queen Margaret, Alexander I and David I, came a Normanisation of the Scottish realm and its administration.

Alexander I (1107-24) gave Perth its earliest burghal status, founded the Abbey of Scone (1114) and kept court within the Old Castle of Perth. During his reign he created at Perth three great offices of state - the Lord High Constable, to head the military; the Justiciar, to oversee the laws; and the Chancellor, Keeper of the Great Seal, to head the Great Council of Earls, Barons and Prelates.

The Lord High Constable's appointment was then given and made in heredity to the family of Moreville of Cunningham.

During the Wars of Independence, a few months after Bannockburn, King Robert the Bruce appointed by Charter of 12th November 1314 Gilbert de la Haya, fifth in descent from William de la Haya, Principal Butler at the Court of Malcolm IV, to be High Constable of Scotland, the office to be in heredity, as it still is, in the family of Hay, Earls of Errol from 1553.

Perth holds the legal status of a Royal Burgh by virtue of certain Crown Charters granted by the Scottish kings from David I (1153), William the Lion (1210), and Robert the Bruce (1317), all confirmed and enumerated under the Great Seal at Holyroodhouse by King James VI in November 1600, and subsequently ratified by 'The Red Parliament' convened at Perth in August 1606.

The precedence of the Royal Burgh of Perth in the roll of Scottish burghs was legally clarified in 1804 by confirmation that, by virtue of its Royal Charters and their ratification by Act of Parliament, the burgh was entitled to precedence second only to Edinburgh.

From the number of Parliaments held in Perth and the frequent residence there of the Monarch and Court came its importance and status among the burghs. Though at the period no town was so nominated the city became virtually the chief or capital city of Scotland.

In 1836 the Court of Session ratified by recorded minute the right of the chief magistrate of Perth to the title of Lord Provost, a title which remained until the reorganisation of local government in 1975.

In early days the chief magistrates tended to be of the neighbouring great families – Ruthven, Charteris, Thriepland, Murray – each of whom maintained his own troop of guards who, with the armed burgesses, could keep law and order within the bounds. Younger sons of these families often established themselves in the trading community as burgesses.

As the burgh's mercantile growth proceeded and the influence of the landed lairds receded, it became necessary for the burgh to form guards to keep watch and ward from amongst their own citizens, in augmentation of the town's officers of whom there were at most five or six at any one time.

In a national context Crown and Parliament, having the duty to defend the Realm, found it necessary to ensure that its subjects, principally the burgesses of its Royal Burghs, maintained and practised arms and acquired martial experience. Hence came the edicts against golf and football in favour of archery and shooting at the Butts – the Weaponshaws – and the nominating of guards to administer them in good order!

In the 'Fair Maid of Perth' Sir Walter Scott suitably defined the historic role of the predecessors of the Constables by putting into the mouth of Simon Glover:-

"I was summoned to take my part in the defence, as my tenure required, and like
that of other craftsmen who are bound to keep watch and ward".

There is a record that in 1466 four gentlemen – John Bingley, Richard Young, John Paterson and John Murdison – were appointed as the constabulary.

King James VI held such an abhorrence of persons carrying arms that he was moved to write in his own hand, in 1598, a letter to the magistrates of the Scottish burghs ordering them to carry out the terms of the Act forbidding the carrying of arms by unauthorised persons "by apprehending and bringing to the magistrates for punishment all persons carrying pistolets and daggeris".

The Monarch's strong feelings on the matter no doubt stemmed from personal experience including the murder of David Rizzio and his own kidnapping as a young boy at Huntingtower Castle. A few years later he was to find himself calling "Help! Murder!" from the turret of Gowrie House in the Speygate of Perth.

The Act of 1617 by King James VI ordained that constables were to be chosen by Commissioners and Justices of the Peace in their quarter sessions throughout the whole country, two at least in every parish... but in all burghs or Free Cities the constables are to be chosen by the magistrates.

The oath to be taken by the constables and the orders for their guidance were detailed in the Act. Apart from the basic duty to keep watch and ward one of the main duties of the constables in the burghs was the cleansing of the streets.

So much importance was attached to such civic duties that over two hundred years later, in 1829, the constables were under the administration of the burgh's Commissioners for Paving and Lighting.

In 1829 the Commissioners, by virtue of the powers vested in them by an amending Act passed in June 1819, appointed an efficient police force within the city under the charge of a superintendent.

In the following year, 1830, the former 'constables' became re-nominated 'High Constables' and in place of 'Preses' nominated their chief officer, Henry Hepburn, 'Moderator' with the Rev. James Esdaile, chaplain; W. Malcolm, M.D., physician; Alex McKenzie, solicitor; and Robert Greig, clerk.

The earliest reference to the maintenance of the police is contained in a minute of the town council dated 4th February 1811 when an intended Bill for 'Paving, Lighting and Cleansing the City and for maintaining Police and Good Order' was discussed. The dung collected on the streets was to be at the disposal of the Commissioners for the defraying of the purposes of the Act!

On 3rd December 1821 it was requested that the town's sergeants be placed under the superintendent of police so that they could be used as day policemen. This was refused!

On 2nd June 1828 the council had received from the Preses of the Committee of the Convention of Royal Burghs the drafts of two General Police Bills intending to apply to all the Royal Burghs in Scotland. After consideration it was decided not to accept these Bills as the council felt that existing Police Acts were sufficient for the City.

On 4th January 1830 'Instructions and Regulations for the Society of High Constables of the City of Perth by The Lord Provost, Magistrates and Council' were made and duly filed in the records of Perth Town Council. These are the first Regulations of the Society and appear at Appendix II.

The formation of The Society of High Constables of the City of Perth thus originates from 1830. The transition from 'Constables' to 'High Constables' is illustrated by the City Lists 1829-30, shown as follows, where Henry Hepburn, for example, was Preses of the constables in 1829 and Moderator of the High Constables in 1830. Many other names appear on both lists but the significance of the order, and initials for some and christian names for others, is not known. No doubt such matters were of great importance at the time.

CITY LISTS (1829)

MAGISTRATES AND TOWN COUNCIL

Robert Ross of Oakbank, Esq. Lord Provost, Sheriff and Coroner;
John Wright, Esq. Dean of Guild
James Norwell   )
John Ross, jun.   ) Esqrs. Merchant Baillies
David Robertson   )
David Clunie, Esq. Trades' Baillie
James Crow, Esq. Treasurer
P.G. Stewart, Esq. late Provost   )
David Beatson   )   )
Thomas Beatson   )   )
John McNaughton)   Esqrs. late Baillies)
Robert Matthews   )   )   Merchant
William Malcom   )   )   Councillors
Arch. Turnbull   )   )
Henry Ballingall   )   Esqrs.   )
Robert Sangster   )   )
Messrs. Robert Buist,   Councillor for the Glovers
   Henry Hepburn,   Councillor for the Small Trades
   Pat. Wallace,   Councillor for the Hammermen
   John McEwen,   Deacon of the Bakers, and Convener of the Trades
   James Cant,   Deacon of the Hammermen
   John McEwan,   ditto of the Bakers
   George Young,   ditto of the Glovers
   Thomas Ritchie,   ditto of the Wrights
   Js. Craigdallie, jun.   ditto of the Tailors
   Thos. Rutherford,   ditto of the Fleshers
   John Graham,   ditto of the Shoemakers
City Clerks – John Miller, Esq; Alex McKenzie, Esq.
Procurator Fiscal for the City – Wm. Wedderspoon, Esq. Office 14 High Street.
City Chamberlain – James Brodie, Esq. No. 1 High Street.

The Town Court sits every Tuesday, and the Council meets the first Monday of every month.

GUILD COURT

John Wright, Esq. Dean of Guild
Robert Ross, Esq. Provost

CONSTABLES 1829

Mr. Henry Hepburn, Preses.   Mr. Robert Greig, Clerk.

John Braid	James Pitcairn	James Miller
Robert Duncan	Thomas Reid	James McLeish
John Middlemiss	John Stewart	John Fergusson
James Christie	James Farney	Robert Abbot
John Menzies	Thomas Dow	Andrew Buik
William Marshall	Peter Campbell	William Peacock
Robert Robertson	Robert Sharpe	James Dewar
James Murie	Arch. Campbell	George Duncanson
Robert Bower	James Brodie	William Dow
Andrew Burns	Alexander Reid	William Gellatly
James Duncan	James Robertson	Andrew Ferrier
David Clunie	James Taylor	A. Wallace, Jun.
William Wighton	Thomas Taylor	W. McKenzie
George Tulloch		

Rev. James Esdaile, Chaplain
W. Malcolm, Esq. M.D. Physician

MEMBER OF PARLIAMENT FOR THE BURGH –
The Hon. Hugh Lindsay of Balcarras.

HIGH CONSTABLES 1830

Henry Hepburn, Esq. Moderator
Rev. James Esdaile, Chaplain
W. Malcolm, M.D. Physician
Alex. McKenzie, Esq. Solicitor
Robert Greig, Esq. Clerk

James Christie	James Taylor	R. Honey
John Menzies	Thomas Taylor	J. Forsyth
William Marshall	James Miller	J. Elrick
Robert Robertson	James McLeish	W. Gorrie
James Murie	John Ferguson	P. Imrie
Robert Bower	Robert Abbot	J. Baird
James Duncan	Andrew Buik	J. Mount
David Clunie	William Peacock	D. Peacock
William Wighton	James Dewar	W. Walker
George Tulloch	George Duncanson	J. McDuff
Thomas Reid	William Dow	A. Greig
John Stewart	William Gellatly	J. Graham
James Farney	A. Wallace, Jun.	J. Deas
Thomas Dow	W. McKenzie	J. Bower
Peter Campbell	R. Matthew	W. Kettles
Arch. Campbell	R. Keay, Jun.	I. McEwan
Alexander Reid		

MEMBER OF PARLIAMENT FOR THE BURGH –
The Hon. Hugh Lindsay of Balcarras.

CHAPTER TWO

THE TRANSITION PERIOD

The creation of a paid constabulary under a superintendent, when acting in consort on occasion with the newly-designated High Constables, appeared to have gone smoothly within the Burgh of Perth.

The situation in Edinburgh had given rise to some friction when the High Constables were moved to petition the Magistrates enquiring "if the batons placed in our hands by your Lordships and Council are to be respected by the Officer appointed by the Superintendent of Police?" It was explained that the Police Act was designed to relieve them of any calls and that the police superintendent, as superior officer, was directly responsible to the council. The explanation given, while accepted, was minuted as "not as conclusive as the members desired". Today the Perth High Constables are invariably escorted by the chief officer of police (a successor to the Superintendents) on their parades in recognition of the link.

It had long been obvious that it was necessary to form an adequate, paid constabulary and Sir Robert Peel's Metropolitan Police reforms of 1830 speedily spread throughout the nation – hence 'Bobbies' and 'Peelers'.

By 1830 the peace of the Burgh was more immediately preserved by the body of police established by Act of Parliament and the city was divided into nine wards with Commissioners and an executive superintendent of police.

An earlier riot on the North Inch in the events leading to the Reform Act 1832 found the few available constables unable to contain the troubles. The magistrates were forced to send for a troop of 4th Queen's Dragoons from Kilmarnock! The whole regiment followed as a permanent garrison and were stabled in the remains of Cromwell's Citadel on the South Inch. This proved inadequate, prompting the building of the barracks at Drumhar in 1795 - to be named 'The Queen's Barracks' until demolished in 1961.

Tangible relics of the 'Constables' pre-1830 still remain in the hands of the Society in the form of batons carrying the Arms of King George III (1760-1820) and King William the IV (1830-1837). *(See illustration).*

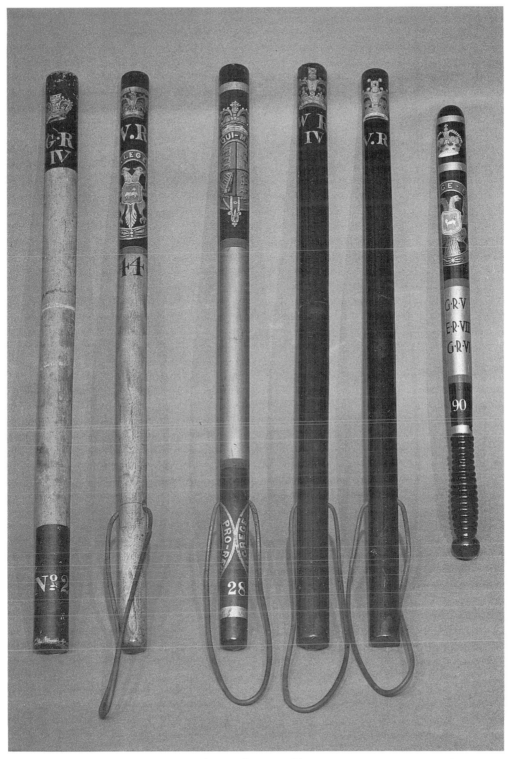

A selection of ceremonial batons

On the occasion of royal visits it was protocol for the Privy Council to order the Earl of Errol, as Lord High Constable, to instruct the Lord Provost and magistrates to arrange for the keeping of good order and guarding of the Monarch.

In 1633 King Charles I, after his Scottish Coronation at Holyroodhouse on 18th June, came from Falkland to Perth. The magistrates, on the instruction of the Lord High Constable, appointed a number of officers, assigned them their duties and provided them with new clothes. On the King's entry he was "conveyit be our young men in guard with partizans, clad in red and whyte, to his ludging at the end of the South Gait (Gowrie's Palace)". This escort was provided by the Glover Incorporation.

But all previous royal visits were eclipsed in general enthusiasm by that of the young Queen Victoria accompanied by Prince Albert on 6th September 1842, and here the recently designated Society of High Constables of the City of Perth served for the first time in a major role as a ceremonial guard. The magistrates took an early opportunity to correspond with the Society in regard to the proceedings.

A meeting of the council and office-bearers was called on receipt of the town clerk's letter. On 20th August John MacFarlane, Moderator, replied to the Lord Provost and Magistrates:-

Perth, 20th August 1842.

Gentlemen - In consequence of your letter to me this morning, the Council of High Constables have deemed it proper to call the body together this evening. It is proposed that, if our services are required in the procession, or if we shall have the honour to move, as attendants, either on your honours or on the Royal cortege, the members should appear in a particular uniform - many of them having already signified their readiness to provide it at their own expense.

The proposal will be submitted to the general meeting this evening at nine o'clock; and it would be very desirable to have something to state distinctly regarding this point. Understanding that you are to meet previously, I should feel obliged by your taking this matter into consideration, and intimating to me your views on the subject, that we may be able to decide as to the adoption and preparation of the uniform without delay.

I have the honour to be, Gentlemen, your most obedient Servant,

(Signed)   John McFarlane,

Moderator, H.C.

To the Lord Provost and Magistrates of Perth.

The same day, at a meeting of all the members of the Society, the council's proposal of the adoption of a particular uniform was considered. The council's recommendation was:-

"Dress coats of forest green with green silk velvet collars, the skirts to be lined with straw-coloured serge or sarcenet, gilt buttons bearing a Royal crown, and that of these, besides the usual number and arrangement, three should appear on each of the cuffs and pocket flaps; vests of cassimere, corresponding in colour with the skirt linings, and black satin stocks for the neck; black cloth trousers of a handsome shape - those of the Council or Office-bearers being ornamented with gold lace along the side-seams; the whole to wear an appropriate silver badge, with favours on the left breast, and white kid gloves on the hands ... each to be armed with a gilded truncheon or baton with the royal shield, scroll and motto, towards the one end, and the City arms near the other."

The town clerk Archibald Reid's letter to the Moderator of 20th August 1842 stated that the magistrates would be most happy to receive the services of the High Constables "either as a Body Guard to Her Majesty the Queen when passing through Perth, or to themselves in case the Queen should be sufficiently protected by the military".

The account of the High Constables' part in the Royal visit was recorded by David Peacock, clerk and treasurer of the society, and published in his "Perth, Its Annals and Its Archives".

QUEEN VICTORIA'S VISIT - 1842

"The High Constables had assembled about noon on the parade adjoining the Council House, in their new uniform and equipments, when the Magistrates took their departure to meet the Queen at Dupplin, and present the City Address. They marched four deep, to the Triumphal Arch, at the extremity of Princes Street, and took up their appointed station immediately within the barrier, on either side, and kept that post for several hours until the return of the civic deputation about five o'clock, when the files opened out and the Magistrates took their places on foot between them, facing the folding gates which were then thrown open, and there awaited the approach of the Royal cortege. Immediately on her Majesty's carriage drawing up in front of the Triumphal Arch the Magistrates advanced - the members of the High Constables defiling to the right and left, and skirting the Royal chariot on either side - while the imposing ceremony of the presentation of the City Keys to the Queen, and the Freedom of the Corporation to Prince Albert, was going on, amid the acclamations of the multitudes who thronged the numerous balconies and platforms, arrayed in their gayest attire. The scene is described by a graphic delineator of the ceremonial as having in it "much of the grand and sublime".

The High Constables advanced in double files on either side - the two front divisions flanking the Magisterial carriages, the two rear companies guarding that of Her Majesty and Prince Albert - the small military escort giving way to the civic columns, and falling back close upon the rear; and thus, although not specially so arranged, the members of the Society actually had the honour of acting as bodyguard to the Queen and her Royal Consort through the streets of our fair and ancient City. The Royal Victoria of Great Britain, the Sovereign of the mightiest and most extensive empire on earth, thus passed through the ancient VICTORIA, amid the acclamations of at least 100,000 of her faithful subjects, with only half-a-dozen Carabineers (three in front and three behind) and two officers as a military escort, being the only military force in or near the city - an instance of Royal confidence and popular loyalty alike honourable to the Queen and her people. As the High Constables had this high honour, it may be nothing more than justice to them here to record the muster-roll on that august occasion.

The active force of the body in the spirit-stirring work of this auspicious day consisted of exactly sixty-eight members, besides John Macfarlane, Esq., Moderator and Commander. Besides these, there were several other members officially engaged at the head of other societies and incorporations, or as members of the Magistracy or Town Council."

First Division – under Captain Croll

Robert Ancell, gunmaker
James Annan, plasterer
William Brisbane, corkcutter
James Brough, joiner
David Cameron, perfumer
William Cameron, builder
Robert Cairnie, bellhanger
Peter Comrie, painter
George Croll, reedmaker (Captain)
John Dall, superindendent of Perth mills

David Dandie, druggist
David Dron, printer
Stewart Duncan, haberdasher
William Cairnie, hatter
William Cuthbert, coachbuilder
James Dewar, woollen-draper
John Dewar, spirit merchant
James Douglas, brassfounder
James Chalmers, woollen-draper

Second Division – under Captain Hewat

Peter Robert Drummond, bookseller
James Duff, cabinetmaker
Buchanan Dunsmore, woollen-draper
Thomas Edward, auctioneer
William Murray Farney, shoemaker
Walter Foyer, hatter
David Gibson, plasterer
Kirkwood Hewat, tallow-chandler (Captain)
William Imrie, leather-merchant

Peter Imrie, cabinetmaker
John Wilson Jameson, banker
Thomas Lennox, grocer
James Fairbairn, engraver
James Gardiner, watchmaker
John Gray, grocer
Alexander Fleming, tailor
James Beatson Isdale, draper
Andrew Heiton, architect

Third Division – under Captain Murie

Alexander Miller, wine-merchant
David Miller, merchant
James Mitchell, grocer
Thomas Menzies, innkeeper
James Morris, collector of harbour dues
David Murie, general agent (Captain)
J. Macfarlane, ironfounder (Moderator)
James Macfarlane, watchmaker
John McGlashan, tool-cutter

John McNab, watchmaker
Richard McLean, bootmaker
Charles Paton, bookseller
David Peacock, music teacher
    (Clerk and Treasurer)
Wm. Pearson, silk-mercer and draper
Joseph Ranson, glass and china merchant
James Ritchie, glass and china merchant

Fourth Division – Under Captain Shedden

Thomas Richardson, bookseller
Donald Robertson, Star Hotel
Robert Hay Robertson, grocer etc.
James Robson, music teacher
David Ross, merchant (Ex-Moderator)
Andrew Roy, grocer
Alexander Scott, writer (Secretary)
Charles Scott, cabinetmaker

Andrew Sharp, baker
Charles Shedden, watchmaker (Captain)
John Storer, merchant
Peter Tait, shoemaker
Alexander Tulloch, tailor and clothier
William Tulloch, saddler
William Watson, shoemaker

These were the only parties, besides the municipal authorities, who had the distinguished honour to take part and move in this memorable pageant."

A print by the Dundee printmaker Gershom Cumming (1810–1898) was issued on 19th January 1843 and appears on the jacket of this book. We are indebted to Perth Museum and Art Gallery for permission to reproduce both the print and part of the description. It was one of the first visual records of the Queen's visit which was available as an individual print rather than of a large and expensive bound volume. It was issued at the modest price of 7/6d (about 38p) for an uncoloured print; coloured ones were double this price.

Cumming's viewpoint allows him to concentrate on the impressive mass of people lining the streets, crowded into balconies and peering through every available window. The various incorporated trades appear behind the arch along the length of Princes Street. One thousand individuals 'of the working classes' had also been enrolled to line the streets and maintain good order. They were paid 2/6d (about 13p), were issued with white rods and had to appear in their Sunday best.

Although the arch appeared to be constructed of sandstone it was actually made of timber covered with canvas and then painted to imitate sandstone. This construction allowed the arch to be built quickly within ten days at a modest cost of £100!

The triumphal arch was designed by the city architect, William MacKenzie, and was considered to be of 'admirably good taste and proportions'. Notice the detailing normally associated with stone construction: the thin even joints between the blocks of stone, the keystones above the arches, the large volutes joining the central arch to the smaller side arches and the dentils (small square blocks) beneath the decorated entablature. Notice also the carvings around the main arch depicting winged figures of Fame blowing trumpets and the arms of the city of Perth on each of the main pillars.

Six years later the Society was called on to provide a more hastily assembled Royal guard.

QUEEN VICTORIA'S VISIT OF 1848

In 1848 Queen Victoria and the Prince Consort had obtained the lease of the old Castle of Balmoral and were to return to London by sea from Aberdeen in September, when very stormy weather caused a quick change of plan which brought the Royal party by carriages to Montrose, the terminus of the railway at the time. A pilot engine arriving at Perth half an hour before the Queen led to the summoning of Mr. Tasker, the resident engineer of the Scottish Central Railway Company, from the hospitable dinner table of Mr. Gloag in Marshall Place. It was said that Her Majesty first enquired if Lord Mansfield was at Scone, but on being told that he was away from home it was indicated that the George Inn would serve very well!

Miss Davidson, the manageress of 'The George', was absent, having in an enthusiasm of loyalty gone off to Aberdeen to witness the Royal embarkation, but the rooms above the Lady Walk facing the river were speedily prepared and Miss Davidson returned before the Royal departure next morning to be personally assured by the Queen that all was well.

A company of The Royal Scots provided the guard at 'The George' and the High Constables turned out next morning with the Magistrates wearing their 1842 court swords. 'The George' subsequently became known as 'The Royal George'.

QUEEN VICTORIA'S VISIT OF 1864

Prince Albert died in 1861 and on August 30th 1864 the widowed Queen came again to Perth in order to inaugurate the statue, by Brodie, of her late Consort. Erected on the North Inch, this was the citizens' tribute to the life and work of the Prince who holds in his hand the plans of the Crystal Palace, erected for the Great Exhibition of 1851 in Hyde Park. The High Constables again provided the guard of honour on the Inch. The demonstrations of loyalty were recorded as "fittingly quiet and subdued". With the Lord Provost and Magistrates were:-

The Earl of Mansfield, Lord Lieutenant; Sir Charles Wood, M.P.; Lord Kinnaird; Viscount Dupplin; Viscount Strathallan; Major-General Walker and the Hon. Arthur Kinnaird, M.P.

This visit was also the subject of a print by Gershom Cumming and again we are indebted to Perth Museum and Art Gallery for permission to reproduce it on the jacket of this book, and for the following description:- "Despite the wish of many Town Council officials and the people of Perth and Perthshire, no permanent memorial was erected to commemorate the Queen's visit to Perth in 1842. In a less happy situation, the Queen did find herself in Perth 22 years later unveiling a statue which was, however, a memorial to her late husband Prince Albert. The statue was the work of the Edinburgh sculptor William Brodie who also chose the location at the edge of the North Inch. The Prince is depicted in the robes of the Order of the Thistle and he holds an open scroll on which the elevation of the Crystal Palace is traced. Prince Albert had followed the architectural matters of his country very closely. The Queen spoke personally to the sculptor after the inauguration ceremony. She praised his skill and the truthfulness of the likeness which he had achieved."

THE 1843 RIOT

It was in May 1843, the year after Queen Victoria's ceremonial entry, that the High Constables had been called out for the last time to assist the Magistrates to quell a major disturbance of the peace.

From '*Perthshire Advertiser*' of lst June 1843, reported the event:-

The Perth High Constables on Active Duty

"The usual peacefulness of our City was exchanged on the evening of Thursday last for a scene of disorder and frightful violence, such as was never before witnessed in Perth, and which is happily rare in this country. On that night a party of the 68th Regiment, who came to occupy our Barracks in the beginning of last winter, may be literally said to have held possession of several of the principal streets for nearly two hours, armed with sticks and bludgeons, assailing all who came in their way, or were unable to get beyond their reach, to the serious and nigh fatal injury of a considerable number of young and old, who were knocked down and cruelly beaten by this band of lawless and infuriated soldiery. About eight o'clock that evening the rioters, to the number of 60 or 70 at least, filled the streets from pavement to pavement, flourishing sticks - many of the sticks being scooped in the head and loaded with lead. Some of them were obviously inflamed with drink, and all were maddened with rage and fury. The citizens were naturally seized with consternation. Shutters were put on, and shops rapidly shut. Up to this time the soldiers encountered little opposition. A small picket came down from the Barracks about half past eight o'clock, but they utterly failed to stop or restrain the rioters. It was near nine o'clock before a sufficient force of Police and High Constables could be got collected, so as to give a reasonable chance of beating them off and clearing the streets. The tables, however, were turned in excellent style. At ten minutes to nine o'clock the Provost and Magistrates, who had hurriedly assembled in the Town Hall, came forth, along with a body of Police Constables and High Constables, armed by their authority with batons, and having reached the end of Watergate and George Street, Provost Sidey read the Riot Act. The moment the Provost finished reading the Riot Act and shouted "Charge", the Constables and others, who were armed as described, sprang forward with an ardour that speedily infused a panic among the rioters. Betwixt the Cross and top of High Street a great number of soldiers were severely punished. Ever and anon a "Red Coat" disappeared among the feet of the pursuers. Thirteen of the rioters were altogether secured and conveyed to the Police Office, most of them bleeding, bruised, and more or less hurt. One was so much hurt that he had to be conveyed to the Infirmary. The courage and promptitude shown by the High Constables, Police, and others on that night, deserve praise and acknowledgement. Prominent among the High Constables on that occasion were the late Mr. Bell, Cabinetmaker; John Storer, Merchant; and Cairnie, Bellhanger.

On 28th July 1843, in the High Court of Justiciary, before Lords Moncrieffe and Medwyn and the Lord Justice Clerk, a sentence of 18 months' imprisonment was passed upon five of the prisoners."

Following Queen Victoria's visit in 1864 a considerable time elapsed before the next Royal occasion. In October of 1913 the Moderator and Council attended the unveiling of the King Edward Memorial in King Edward Street and the next Royal visit was on 10th July 1914 when King George V and Queen Mary and Princess Mary came to Perth to open the new Perth Royal Infirmary at Tullylumb. The High Constables mounted the guard of honour, and the members were formed up outside the Municipal Building by Sergeant Quade of the 3rd Black Watch. Then they marched in procession by way of High Street, Methven Street, King Street and King's Place to the square at the entrance to the General Station as an escort to the Lord Provost, Magistrates and Town Council. (*See illustration*).

King George V and Queen Mary at Perth station on 10th July 1914
after opening the new Perth Royal Infirmary at Tullylumb

The members of the Society and the Atholl Highlanders formed the Guard of Honour and were formed up in one semi-circle between the Station Hotel entrance and the platform at which their Majesties were to be received. As the Royal Party entered the square from the station a Royal Salute was given by the Society.

Among those presented were the Moderator and Mrs Shaw. After the presentation the Guard of Honour was inspected by His Majesty the King. On the return from the Infirmary the Royal Salute was again given by the Guard of Honour and after their departure the members marched to the Station Hotel where at the call of the Moderator the toasts of the King and Queen and Royal Family were loyally pledged.

CHAPTER THREE

ANNUAL OUTINGS, SOCIAL AND SPORTING ACTIVITIES

Mention of drill parades runs like a thread through the early Society minutes and regulations. In those of December 1884 there is a reference to the commencement of drill about the beginning of February and presumably by then an annual routine; an 1891 notice confirms the point. *(See Frontispiece illustration).*

In November 1886 "the members then present were for the space of an hour exercised in military drill." Ten years later it was resolved that a "drill be held at least four times a year and should take place in the first week of every quarter." An honorary drill instructor was appointed.

It is perhaps worth relating that as recently as 1990 it was raised in Council that drill parades would help to smarten the appearance of High Constables on Armistice Sunday and at the Kirking of the Council. The suggestion received little support!

By June 1885 the Society was involved in annual excursions and a party went by the North British Railway to Burntisland. They then travelled by the steamer "Stirling Castle" to Stirling and returned to Perth by cab and railway.

In June 1895 the annual excursion was made to Roslin and on return to Edinburgh the Society "was sumptuously entertained by the Moderator of the High Constables of Edinburgh." It was noted that "letters of mutual good fellowship have since passed between the two Societies."

On 24th June 1896 the annual excursion "in accordance with the resolution" was made to Aberfeldy by rail, thence by coach to Taymouth Castle. The Society was conducted over the castle by Mr Dun, factor, and the housekeeper, thence they proceeded by Kenmore to Fortingall where they dined before visiting Castle Menzies. After tea at Weem they were shown over the castle by the housekeeper. A crowded day ended with the Society returning to Perth "all highly pleased with the excursion".

By September 1895 a golf match had taken place on the links at Leven between members of the Societies of Perth and Edinburgh - "Edinburgh having gained."

The Moderator intimated on 5th March 1894 that on the occasion of their Annual Dinner in December the Moderator and Council of the Edinburgh High Constables had presented the

Society with a very handsome silver-mounted Ram's Head. *(See illustration)*.

The Moderator spoke in warm terms of the long and close relationship which had existed between the two sister societies of Edinburgh and Perth - "a friendship of which this magnificent present was not the only, though the latest, token." He was sure the Society fully reciprocated this warm friendship and hoped it would long continue.

On 2nd December 1895 the Moderator referred to the formation of a Golf Club in connection with the Society and suggested a committee be formed. A bowling match was arranged with the Edinburgh Society on the Perth club's green for 15th August 1906.

In 1904 an outing was arranged to Balmoral where photographs were taken of both the group and the Council. *(See illustrations)*.

On 29th May 1912 the Edinburgh High Constables invited the Perth Society to an annual golf match in Edinburgh. The following year both the golf and bowling matches with Edinburgh had been successful from the Perth point of view with the Edinburgh Society's golf trophy coming to the city.

A curling section was founded on 18th March 1923 and the following year a trophy was purchased by the Council for annual competition.

In 1931 there was a trip to Oban and Loch Creran *(see illustrations)* and although there were many annual outings between the two World Wars thereafter they became less popular and are now exceedingly rare. Chapter 7 gives details of the most recent ones.

The Ram's Head Snuff Mull
presented by the High Constables of Edinburgh in 1893

Outing to Balmoral, 1904; members, families and friends.

The Council at Balmoral, 1904, with Lord Provost Thomas Love and Moderator
Robert Keay 2nd. and 3rd. from left in the back row

CHAPTER FOUR

FIRST WORLD WAR 1914-1918

The outbreak of the 1914-1918 war affected the role and duties of the Society. This is best illustrated by extracts from the Society's minutes of the period.

25th August 1914.

The Secretary reported that at the request of the Chief Constable, and with the approval of the Moderator, he had called upon the members to serve during the day in watching the three water reservoirs at Muirhall, Parkhead and Viewlands.

26th August 1914.

Lord Provost Scott attended and explained to the meeting the result of the meeting of Magistrates today and as to certain difficulties which had occurred to them in regard to the right and authority of the Society under its present instructions as well as the oath taken by members in view of the appointment of Special Constables which was being arranged for by Parliament. Without entering into the merits of the matter the Council considered that it would be well to ascertain full information as to the appointment of Special Constables before the Society took any definite steps, and the Lord Provost agreed to submit such information to the Society as soon as he was in a position to do so. The Lord Provost approved of it being an instruction from the Council to the members that they should in the present crisis wear their official Badge of Office, in order that they could be readily identified by the Chief Constable and his men at any time they required assistance. On the suggestion of the Moderator, the Council agreed to recommend the members to make a donation from the funds of £10 to the National Relief Fund.

The Moderator explained to the members that as soon as the War broke out he and the Secretary had got in touch with the Lord Provost and Chief Constable and had offered the services of the members for whatever duty might be required of them and that following thereon the members to the number of 30 per day had been on duty watching the City's reservoirs from Saturday 22nd instant and that this meeting had been called to come to an arrangement as to continuing this duty or undertaking others but that in view of the contemplated appointment of Special Constables, the Lord Provost and Magistrates had some difficulty in the matter.

5th September 1914.

It was explained to the meeting by the Moderator that no further information in regard to the appointment and duties of the Special Constables had been received from the Lord Provost but that it had been ascertained from the Chief Constable that these when enrolled would be on a similar footing to the ordinary Police Constables and would require to take regular duty either by day or night if called upon. After full consideration of the matter and in respect that the majority of the members of the Society were men in professions and businesses, who could not be expected to undertake such obligations at the risk of neglecting their own affairs, which was also a necessary duty at the present time, the Council were unanimously of the opinion that they could not be called upon or expect the members to enrol as Special Constables and they considered that the value of their services would be as great under their ordinary powers and duties as members of the Society.

7th September 1914.

The Moderator reported to the Meeting that Ex-Bailie and Councillor McPherson had agreed to become his successor in the office of Moderator but that as the regulations provided that a member of the Town Council could not become an office-bearer of the Society it would be necessary to ask the Magistrates to have the rule suspended for Mr. McPherson's term of office. The Meeting cordially approved of Mr. McPherson's appointment.

10th September 1914.

The Secretary read a letter from the Town Clerk intimating that the Magistrates, in terms of the Society' request, suspended the rule.

15th September 1914.

It was unanimously resolved to suggest at the meeting tonight that a subscription be taken from the members present for the Belgian Relief Fund. Amount collected was £5.

7th October 1914.

Arrangements for proposed Jumble Sale for the benefit of the soldiers engaged in the present War were discussed and considered. There was read to the Meeting a letter from the Secretary of the Perth City & County Recruiting Association requesting the Society to co-operate in a Procession and Demonstration proposed to be held this month for the object of stimulating Recruiting. The Council unanimously agreed to fall in with the proposal. A letter from Messrs. David McGregor & Company, Jewellers, with accompanying design for an Ex-Moderators' Badge was submitted to the Meeting and after consideration the Secretary was requested to order seven Badges at a cost of one pound five shillings each as quoted in his letter.

24th October 1914.

Sixty members of the Society assembled at 2.30 p.m. After being formed up at the Albert Monument by Mr. George Baird as the instructor they marched to their position in front of the Academy along with the other bodies taking part in the procession and demonstration organised by the Perth City & County Recruiting Association. At 3.00 p.m the different regiments, societies and other bodies marched in procession led by the Society of High Constables by way of Charlotte Street, George Street, High Street, Caledonian Road and York Place to the Old Infirmary which was occupied by the wounded Belgian soldiers. There a halt was made and the Belgian anthem played by the bands, and cheers given for the Belgians. *(See illustrations).*

Members parading on the North Inch before a Recruiting March
through the the City, 24th October 1914

The March in full swing preceded by the High Constables

The same March

16th December 1914.

The members of the Society held a supper and smoker in the Salutation Hotel this evening when the past Moderators still surviving were presented with special and suitable Badges and when the Hon. Drill Instructor, Mr. George Baird, was presented by the Society with a Sheraton Timepiece. There was also presented to the Ex-Moderator a silver tea and coffee service on silver tray with suitable inscription which had been subscribed for by the members as a mark of appreciation of the services of Ex-Moderator and Mrs. Shaw during the specially strenuous time in which he held office.

26th February 1915.

On account of the City Hall being occupied by the Army Service Corps the Council resolved that the drills appointed at the last meeting would require to be deferred.

2nd December 1918.

The Moderator referred to the work done by the High Constables during the War. He spoke of the splendid spirit which animated those who took part in such work as guarding reservoirs and drilling and of that generosity which enabled them to raise over £400 for patriotic purposes. The Moderator said that six or seven members joined the colours at the beginning of the War, before conscription was introduced, which was proof enough of their patriotism and was a record of which the Society might well be proud.

CHAPTER FIVE

1918-1939

Links with the sister Societies were renewed in the post-war period and in March 1923 the Moderator, Andrew Miller, along with the Secretary, attended the Annual Dinner of the High Constables of Holyroodhouse. The Moderator also attended the dinner of the High Constabulary of the Port of Leith and "had been received with the usual kindness and courtesy by these august bodies."

By 1926 the subscription had been raised to one guinea!

A special occasion was noted on 7th November 1926 when the members marched from the Burgh Court Room to St John's Church where a special dedication service was held. A Memorial to the 40 members of the Middle Church who gave their lives in the Great War was unveiled by Lord Provost Dempster.

An interesting record of continuity took place in 1928 when Walter Stuart was elected to his term as Moderator. His father, Charles C. Stuart, had held office from 1866-68 while his maternal grandfather, David Murie, occupied the chair from 1848-50. His son, Kenneth Stuart, and his grandson, Walter Stuart, were also members of the Society.

The King's illness resulted in a telegram being sent by the Society on 19th December 1927 to the Queen at Buckingham Palace. "The Society of High Constables of Perth at their annual dinner in the Station Hotel humbly offer their respectful sympathy with Her Majesty The Queen and the other members of the Royal Family at this time of anxiety and earnestly hope for the complete recovery of His Majesty The King."

Happily, the Society was able in 1931, just before setting off on their annual excursion to Oban and Loch Creran, to submit their loyal felicitations on the King's birthday. One of those on the boat trip, in the check suit with matching hat, was the well known member and Perth tobacconist Charles Rattray, whose contributions when Custodier are mentioned elsewhere. *(See illustration).*

On 6th May 1935 the nation was able to celebrate the Silver Jubilee of the Accession of King George V. Members of the Society attended the thanksgiving service in St John's Church and the drumhead service at Muirton Park.

The annual outing in 1931, to Oban and Loch Creran; at Oban Station

On Loch Creran, 1931; Charles Rattray in the check suit and cap.

Another Royal occasion for the Society took place on 10th May 1935 when their Royal Highnesses, the Duke and Duchess of York, were presented with the Freedom of the City. They formally opened the new Perth Art Gallery and Museum in George Street and the ceremony took place outside the gallery. High Constables, marshalled by Major James Hepburn, formed the inner bodyguard at the south side by which their Royal Highnesses passed. *(See illustration).*

On the conclusion of the Freedom Ceremony the High Constables re-formed and the Royal couple passed through their ranks on the way to perform the opening ceremony. The High Constables then marched and formed the inner bodyguard for the Royal car to leave at the end of their inspection of the gallery.

The High Constables were again on duty on 23rd January 1936 when they paraded as a guard at the Proclamation of the Accession of King Edward VIII. This was made at the King Edward VII Memorial - a replica of the Mercat Cross in King Edward Street - the first time such a ceremony was held there and a departure from the High Street Cross site.

Five days later a memorial service to King George V was held in St John's Kirk and the High Constables paraded in attendance on the Lord Provost, Magistrates and Council.

Long Service membership was recognised in March 1936 and the Council agreed that members with 30 years' service should have a bar attached to the official badge. Nowadays it is only 25 years before a member's ceremonial baton is inscribed and becomes his personal property.

The subject of drills again occupied the Society and on 7th December 1936 there was discussion regarding marshalling and parading of the Society at ceremonial functions. It was remitted to the Secretary to consult the Lord Provost and Town Clerk regarding the appointment of a Marshal. As far as drills are concerned, it was decided to hold them in February and October 1937.

There was another Royal occasion on 14th December 1936 when the Society attended the Proclamation of the Accession of King George VI at the Mercat Cross in King Edward Street. After assembling at the County Buildings, Tay Street, members marched via South Street to King Edward Street. After the ceremony they returned by the same route and were dismissed.

The Rev. Walter Lee resigned as Chaplain to the society in February 1938 and on 3rd May was succeeded by the Rev. W. A. Smellie B.D.

War again interrupted the affairs of the Society and on 4th September 1939 it was agreed that owing to the national situation the present office bearers should remain in office meantime.

Certain arrangements were made for the duration of the 1939-45 War and these included the discontinuance of all social functions. The Regalia was deposited in the bank for safe keeping. On 5th June 1944 the society was able to congratulate one of their own number when Sir Thomas Hunter M.P. had the honour of knighthood conferred upon by him by the King.

T.R.H.s the Duke and Duchess of York
opening the new Perth Art Gallery and Museum in George Street
after accepting the Freedom of the City on 10th May 1935.

CHAPTER SIX

THE POST-WAR YEARS

1945-1970

The austerity of the Second World War years gave way to a succession of local events in which the High Constables played their part. One of the most spectacular happened on 17th July 1947 when Queen Elizabeth, Colonel-in-Chief of The Black Watch (RHR) visited the city for the presentation of the Freedom to the regiment and to Field Marshal Lord Wavell. The Queen was herself a Freeman since 1935.

The ceremony took place on the North Inch in brilliant weather with the High Constables first in place at the General Station for Her Majesty's arrival. The 40 members of the Society in full regalia and carrying their batons were formed up as a guard of honour and paraded again in the afternoon at the City Chambers.

Duty called again when the great war leader, the Rt. Hon. Winston S. Churchill, came to Perth on 27th May 1948 to be made a Freeman of the city. High Constables were on parade at the ceremony in the City Hall.

That same year new Regulations were adopted and included the following: "On admission, each member will be supplied with a large and small baton. These batons are the property of the Society and on a member ceasing to remain a member of the Society, they must be returned to the Custodier. The Moderator, ex-Moderator, Captains, Secretary and Custodier will hold office for a period of two years and with the exception of the Moderator, will not be eligible for re-election until a further two years has elapsed."

By November that year the Society was up to its full strength of 150.

An interesting event occurred on 4th September 1950 when "The Moderator expressed the Society's deep appreciation to Custodier Charles Rattray for his splendid work over so many years and for the magnificent way in which the new property book had been made into a work of art. Mr. Rattray's name would go down in the Society's annals and the meeting, in enthusiastic response, agreed that a special record be made in the minutes."

A guard of honour from the Society was mounted later that month to welcome H.R.H. Princess Margaret at the City Chambers and at Bowerswell Memorial Home which she officially opened. The House and the bungalows in the grounds served as the city's memorial to those who died in the Second World War. *(See illustration)*.

There was an interesting and very recent sequel when H.R.H.Princess Margaret returned on 15th May 1992 to open an extension to Bowerswell Memorial Home and two of our members on parade, Graham Mitchell and George S.M.Rhodes, had performed a similar duty in September 1950.

A future Queen came to Perth in May 1951 on the occasion of the Festival of Britain. H.R.H. Princess Elizabeth was provided with a guard of honour from the Society at the Station Square and at the Art Gallery. She later saw a performance of Shakespeare's "Twelfth Night" at Perth Theatre.

Nine months later the High Constables were again on duty under totally different circumstances when they attended the Lord Provost, Magistrates and Councillors at the Proclamation ceremony at the Mercat Cross, King Edward Street to announce the Accession of Queen Elizabeth II.

A service in St. John's Kirk followed a week later on 15th February 1952 to mark the memory of his late Majesty King George VI with the High Constables forming a guard.

H.R.H. Princess Margaret opens the Bowerswell Memorial Homes
on 19th September 1950.

Sir Anthony Eden, later Lord Avon, is made a Freeman of the City,
16th May 1956.

It was the Secretary who suggested on 3rd March that on all future ceremonial parades, except the Kirking of the Council, orders and decorations should be worn. This was agreed.

The same meeting also agreed that a telegram should be sent to the Queen on her accession, extending heartfelt sympathy to Her Majesty and all members of the Royal Family and assuring the continual allegiance to the throne of the Society of High Constables of the City of Perth.

The month had not been completed when the Society was again on duty in St. John's Kirk at a service held as a memorial on the funeral of Her late Majesty Queen Mary.

The sadness and solemnity of these occasions were swept away on 2nd June 1953 with the Coronation of the young Queen Elizabeth. The city's celebrations started with a parade of the military and other uniformed organisations in King Edward Street. The High Constables provided the guard of honour at the saluting base and then accompanied the Lord Provost, Magistrates and Councillors to the service in St. John's Kirk and afterwards to the City Chambers. As the personal guests of the Lord Provost the members of the Society joined with the Town Council in pledging the Sovereign's health in the traditional manner.

The Queen Mother returned to Perth in February 1955 and unveiled a stained glass memorial window in St. John's Kirk to the officers and men of The Black Watch who had fallen in World War II. The High Constables formed a guard to Her Majesty at the City Chambers.

Glittering local occasions continued and on 16th May 1956 the High Constables attended on Sir Anthony Eden, wartime foreign secretary and later prime minister, who was made a Freeman of the city at a ceremony in the City Hall. *(See illustration).*

It was a special day in the Society's history on 12th December that year when the Moderator, Secretary and Custodier attended a luncheon given by General Accident Fire and Life Assurance Corporation when a new gavel and tray embellished by silver mountings were presented to the Society. The tray and gavel were made from a piece of bog oak found 18 feet below the Watergate during an excavation by Dr. Margaret Stewart. At that time General Accident were extending their High Street headquarters.

The presentation was made by Sir Stanley Norie Miller. It was noted that this took place on the 50th anniversary of the presentation of the original gavel by the late Sir Francis Norie Miller. The new gavel was a valuable addition to the Society's treasures and perpetuated a link with the great insurance corporation.

Another Royal occasion happened on 10th October 1960 when Her Majesty officially opened the new Queen's Bridge over the River Tay. The complement of 56 High Constables was divided into three new guards. Number one guard was mounted at the City Chambers for the arrival and departure of the Queen. Number two was at the Station Hotel for both arrival and departure with the third guard on duty at the bridge for the opening ceremony. *(See illustration)*.

It was noted that the Society's participation had provided a distinguished background to a memorable occasion.

The Moderator had the honour of being a guest at the Station Hotel lunch and of being presented to Her Majesty and the Duke of Edinburgh who showed a lively interest in the functions of the Society.

The Queen and H.R.H. Prince Philip opening the Queen's Bridge
on 10th October 1960, with Lord Provost John Young
and the Head Boy of Perth Academy, Alistair Cruickshank.

*Kirking of the Council, May 1961, with Moderator William F. Rodger
and Lord Provost John Young, preceded by Town Officer Bert Crawford*

Sport has always played an important part in the affairs of the Society and there was rejoicing at the September 1961 quarterly meeting when it was announced that Perth had beaten the Society of High Constables of Edinburgh at Bruntsfield in the annual golf match. The victory on June 14 had resulted in Perth winning the trophy for the first time since 1956.

There was also good news for the anglers that year with Perth retaining the trophy in two competitions with the Edinburgh Society on 5th June and 10th July. The year was completed with success over Edinburgh in curling.

The year ended for the Society in an important occasion for the High Constables of Edinburgh who were celebrating their 350th anniversary with a dinner in the North British Hotel. The Moderator together with Lord Provost J.T. Young, ex-Lord Provost J.A. Smart, Councillor J.L. Brown and the Secretary attended.

At the request of the Lord Provost the Society provided guards of honour on 2nd September 1962 when the Queen Mother visited the city to commemorate her 25 years as Colonel-in-Chief of The Black Watch. The Society paraded at the City Chambers and at the Art Gallery where all those involved were entertained to afternoon tea by the civic authority.

Moderator William F. Rodger was presented to Her Majesty who expressed great interest in the Society and later, with the Lord Provost, inspected the Society's regalia in the City Chambers.

The death of Sir Winston Churchill resulted in the Society being on parade to accompany the Town Council to church on 29th January 1965.

A lighter moment was to follow that spring when Princess Alexandra came to Perth for the inauguration of the new water works at Gowans Terrace. The Society provided the guard on 12th April. *(See illustration).*

The Annual General Meeting of 1965 decided that the maximum membership should be 100 instead of the then figure of 120 and the previous figure of 150.

There was a further small change in September 1967 when Moderator Tom Caird, on demitting office, proposed the appointment of a Vice-Moderator and that the Society should wear its own tie instead of a black tie at official parades.

At the Moderator's reception prior to the 1969 dinner Vice-Moderator Andrew A. Gellatly was presented with his badge of office. It was gifted to the Society by ex-Moderator J.K. Cairncross.

Additions to the Society's possessions continued and in June 1970 the Custodier received a George IV baton donated by Chief Superintendent Alexander J. Harrower. Mr. Harrower, now retired, had the distinction of being the only police officer ever to serve in the High Constables to date.

1970–1980

The Society provided a guard of honour to the Lord Provost, Magistrates and Council at the Service of Inauguration and Dedication for the first Perth Festival of the Arts on 16th April 1972.

Local Government Reform was on its way in September 1972 and Mr. David K. Thomson enquired if the Council had come to any conclusions with regard to the functions of the Society following reorganisation. The moves would result in Perth having a Provost instead of a Lord Provost. The Moderator replied that the council were awaiting more details of the likely position before formulating their recommendations.

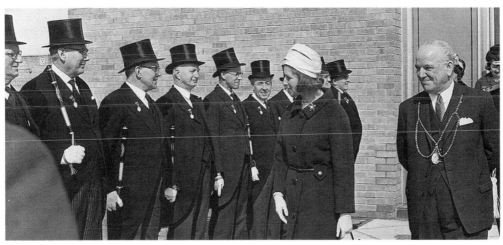

H.R.H. Princess Alexandra and Lord Provost Robert Ritchie
opening Perth Waterworks on 12th April 1965.

The position had become clearer by 4th March 1974 and the Moderator reported on a meeting with the Lord Provost and Town Clerk regarding the future of the Society following reorganisation. It was also proposed that the Society would continue to attend the service for the Kirking of the District Council and Dedication for the Common Good, and the Remembrance Day service. *(See illustration).*

Kirking of the Council, May 1974, with the last Lord Provost of Perth,
Alastair Cross, Moderator David Martin, and Town Officers
Bert Crawford and John Mitchell.

It was also approved in principle that the Society should have a Church Parade of its own every second year to coincide with the installation of the new Moderator. After discussion these items were approved and ex-Lord Provost David K. Thomson also suggested that the Society offer its services as the guard of honour to the Provost of the Perth and Kinross District Council once this body was formed.

The future of the Society was ensured by 3rd March 1975 when the Moderator notified members of the arrangements agreed with Perth and Kinross District Council. The role of the Magistrates would be taken on by the District Council from 15th May 1975. The traditional role at the Kirking of the Council and Remembrance Day Parades would continue, with the Society's name and existing qualifications for membership remaining unchanged. The Society might require to provide an escort for the District Council in parts of the district other than the City of Perth on occasional ceremonial parades.

More arrangements for the future were revealed on 25th April when a letter from the Town Clerk conveyed the Magistrates' approval of the Society's proposals coupled with the request that if possible the Society should continue to use the city's crest.

The end of an era was also marked on 4th May when Perth Town Council gifted a commemorative window to St. John's Kirk with the Society in attendance.

On 25th October 1976 a former Lord Provost of Perth, Sir Robert Nimmo, was sent a letter of congratulation to mark his 50 years' membership of the Society.

With local government reorganisation now firmly established it was back to a Royal occasion for the Society on 7th March 1977. Her Majesty the Queen visited Perth as part of the Silver Jubilee celebrations. At the request of Major David Butter, Lord Lieutenant of Perth and Kinross District, the Society was invited to form two guards of honour. One was at the District Council offices and the other at St. John's Kirk. The Moderator, J. Morris Wood and Mrs. Wood, were presented to Her Majesty at the Council Chambers.

One of Perth's most distinguished sons, Marshal of the Royal Air Force Sir Neil Cameron, became a Freeman of Perth and Kinross District on 26th August 1978. The Society provided the guard of honour at the City Hall. Sir Neil, later Lord Cameron, created history by becoming the first Freeman of the new Perth and Kinross District.

CHAPTER SEVEN

KINDRED SOCIETIES, THE PRESENT AND THE FUTURE

BY

C. ROGER P. WARD, MODERATOR 1989/91

KINDRED SOCIETIES

No history of our own society would be complete without mentioning the High Constables of Holyrood, Edinburgh and Leith. There has long been constant amicable rivalry as to which Society is the oldest and although we claim this honour on the balance of probabilities positive proof is impossible so it continues to be a friendly talking point.

The High Constables and Guard of Honour of Holyroodhouse are the smallest Society with 30 members and are answerable to the hereditary keeper or Baillie of Holyrood, the Duke of Hamilton. They undertake ceremonial duties within the Palace of Holyrood, and the surrounding park, when the monarch is present or is represented.

The High Constables of Edinburgh are the largest society with 276 members split into 23 wards and have a well documented history from 1617 when James VI made his final departure to London. As Edinburgh grew in size a number of societies in adjacent areas were absorbed, including Canongate, Calton and Portobello, which accounts for their large numbers.

The High Constabulary for the Port of Leith, with 50 members, also has a recorded history from the 17th century and although their duties were very similar to those of the Edinburgh Constables it was a port and for that reason had additional duties including the suppression of piracy and of smuggling. They also dealt with excise, weights and measures and the billeting of troops passing through the port. The Port of Leith was absorbed by Edinburgh in 1920 but the Society retained its independence by becoming the bodyguard to the chairman of the Leith Dock Commission, which was later absorbed by the Forth Port Authority. They attend proclamations at the Shore of Leith and ceremonial occasions within the Port of Leith.

1980 to 1992

In April 1981 it was realised that our regalia was both irreplaceable and probably under-insured so we had it photographed, including the silver hallmarks.

On 30th October 1982 we carried ceremonial batons for one of our members, ex-Lord Provost David K. Thomson, who was awarded the Freedom of the District. In 1983 we resurrected the custom of the annual trip and went to Pitlochry Festival Theatre to see "Rookery

Nook". There are many photographs of previous annual trips, between the two world wars, but they now seem less popular in these days of instant transport and communication. We had one more, in June 1990, to a medieval banquet at Dalhousie Courte, but at a quarterly meeting in 1991 the Moderator was the only person in favour of continuing the idea so it was dropped!

In September 1985 a presentation was made to Bert Crawford who had been for 30 years the Town Officer and, with his colleagues, had given invaluable service to the Society.

It was in March 1986 that Council realised Perth was the only one of the four Societies not to have a history and they decided to do something about it. These things take time but it is hoped that the result will be of interest to existing members, and to those who become involved with the Society from time to time, and even to the public at large.

On 7th December l987 six members achieved 40 years of membership; Graham Mitchell, George S. M. Rhodes, D. Beaton Lindsay, Andrew Gellatly, John Darroch and George Valentine. Provost Matheson very kindly entertained them in the City Chambers with other members of the Society.

In May 1991 the members had gathered outside what is now the Ferguson Art Gallery for a group photograph when a penguin passed before our eyes. The identity of this wit remains a mystery but he (or she) certainly enlivened the morning and deserves our thanks! *(See illustration)*.

The Penguin at the group photograph in May 1991, identity unknown...

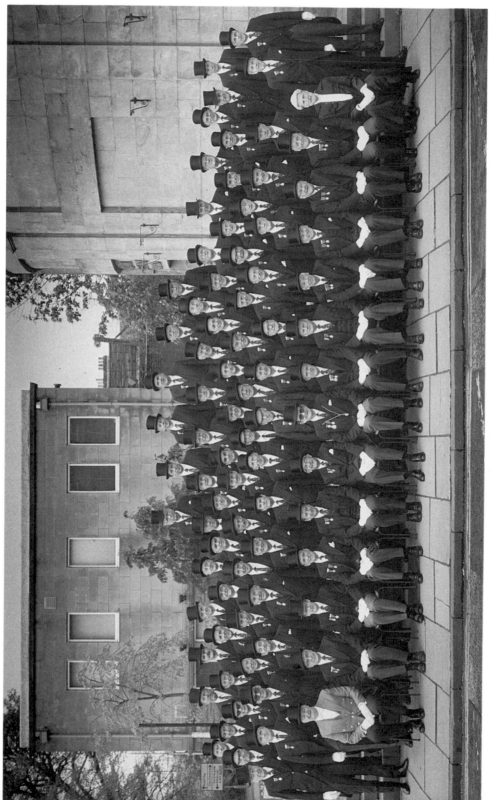

Group photograph, May 1991

THE PRESENT

In addition to escorting the Provost and Councillors every year at the Kirking of the Council in May, on Remembrance Sunday in November, and more recently at the St. Andrew's Day Youth Service, and nowadays only very occasionally visiting Royalty, we have four quarterly meetings and our annual dinner on the second Wednesday in December.

At present our annual membership costs £33 and includes a seat at the dinner, which has an average attendance of about 200. It is fair to say that the annual dinner is the highlight of the Perth social scene and white tie and tails are still worn by the top table. We did discuss changing to black tie in 1989 but the membership voted to maintain the status quo for the time being, and for as long as it is possible to acquire such attire and have it properly laundered and starched! We have eight speeches, two intervals, and the proceedings last from 6.00 p.m. till about 11.30 p.m. – a long evening but shorter than it used to be. From a 1951 menu I see there were twelve speeches so we are improving.

On 14th December 1875, however, the Perthshire Courier gave a detailed report of one of our dinners at which there were 34 speeches, two songs, a 16 verse song with chorus entitled "The Natural History of the High Constables of Perth", and it is said that the proceedings usually lasted from 4.00 p.m. to 4.00 a.m. – as indeed they must have done. In 1877 there were again well over 30 speeches and seven songs, as the menu confirms. *(See illustration).*

It may be that one interval would suffice, or we could reduce still further the number of toasts, or, at the risk of ill-manners, we could devise a system which ensured that the speakers kept to their allotted time...

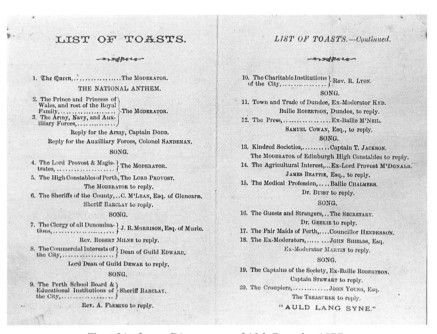

Toast List from a Dinner menu of 13th December 1877.

In 1989 breaking an all male tradition we invited Lady Dunpark to speak and we also had as our guest Flying Officer Erica Landy, ADC to Air Vice Marshal Jim Morris, Air Officer Scotland and Northern Ireland; and in 1990 we welcomed women Councillors for the first time. I believe, as do Council, that in this day and age people should be treated as people, male or female, on their merits without tokenism, and our policy is quite clear; female Provosts, female Councillors, and official female guests of the Society will always be made most welcome.

The last two years have been particularly busy for we have amended our Regulations and these were approved by Perth and Kinross District Council on 20th March 1991 and appear at Appendix III. It was some 40 years since the last major revision so the opportunity was taken to tidy them up, to modernise the wording and to incorporate some new items. These included the power to exclude from membership those who did not attend any of four consecutive meetings or parades, except for ministers of religion; objects which now specifically include social and charitable matters as well as ceremonial; and a Preamble which explains some of our historical origins. We still exist, however, "at the pleasure of the Provost and Councillors of Perth and Kinross District Council".

We have also set out guidelines for the introduction of new members, who must be proposed and seconded in the usual way; be living or working in Perth or its immediate vicinity; be of an age that will enable them to make an active contribution to the affairs of the Society and to continue in service for a reasonable period of time; be prepared to attend regularly; be in possession of the correct dress for parades and should come from all walks of life.

Annual dinner, 1991; top table with Moderator Donald P. McDonald

Presentation of small baton to Sean Liam Fleming by Moderator Roger Ward
on St. Andrew's Day 1989 to mark the first St. Andrew's Day Youth service.

Since 1989, at the particular request of the Provost, we have been on parade at a new St. Andrew's Day Youth Service, to which all youth organisations in the city were invited to send representatives. We felt that for one of the oldest of Perth's traditions to be involved with some of the youngest, in a service dedicated to youth, on the first Sunday in Advent, was particularly appropriate and to mark the occasion small Society batons, suitably inscribed, were presented to Sean Liam Fleming and Laura Jane Ballantine, who were christened at the Services in 1989 and 1990 respectively. *(See illustration).*

In 1990 four members achieved 40 years of membership, James K. Cairncross, Harvey Cruickshank, Alfred J. Smith and William F. Rodger, and the Provost kindly invited them and members of Council to the city chambers to celebrate the occasion.

THE FUTURE

In the 1990s the fabric of society is becoming frayed, changing colour, wearing out, and the threads need to be picked out and reworked and repaired and rejuvenated because no longer is tradition sacrosanct, particularly if it is just for tradition's sake. I have said frequently that privileges bring responsibilities and nowhere is this more true than in our Society. My personal view is that a tradition, to be kept alive and healthy, must have three things, namely a purpose – in our case to escort the Monarch or the Provost and Councillors, fellowship – our quarterly meetings, our parades and our annual dinner, and flexibility – a willingness from time to time to take on new responsibilities. Although our Regulations now include charitable and social objects it could fairly be said that we have not yet found a substantive role for the 1990s, but there is time to do so. Our new Regulations have already improved attendance, our guidelines should ensure a lowering of the average age, and from the enthusiasm of comparative youth will spring ideas.

Whether they include women members or sending the youth of the city to Outward Bound courses or contributing to a worthy local cause worries me not; a far greater danger is apathy.

All four Societies of High Constables are something of an anachronism in this day and age but they nevertheless have a part to play. In the United Kingdom, society as a whole is full of anachronisms, full of quaint costumes and quaint customs, yet we are, in a sense, the cement that binds, the plaster that holds, in fact the rock on which so much of our national heritage stands. We are the traditionalists, the silent majority, the good men and true, who believe that the bread of the 1990s needs leavening with people and with traditions which, harmless in themselves, can set an example of stability in an age when selfishness, militancy and self interest are all too obviously in vogue.

I leave you with the words of Edmund Burke who said 200 years ago something which is every bit as true today – "all that is necessary for the triumph of evil is that good men do nothing". All four bodies of High Constables in that sense do something; they stand for the preservation of peace, justice, law and order. Long may it continue thus!

The annual dinner 1991; l. to r. the Lord Lieutenant, Major Sir David Butter, Provost Alex Murray, Moderator Donald P. McDonald, Principal Speaker Mr. Alistair M. Hamilton and Sir Nicholas Fairbairn, M.P. for Perth and Kinross.

APPENDIX I

THE REGALIA

Each year at the Society's dinner it is the task of the Custodier to ensure that the regalia and trophies in the possession of the Society are displayed. Each part of the regalia has its appointed place.

The most important pieces are normally kept in the district council headquarters in the handsome mahogany cabinet which was designed by Ex-Moderator W. Erskine Thomson and gifted to the society by Ex-Custodier Charles Rattray in 1949.

The most significant piece is the Ram's Head Snuff Mull which is transported to the dinner in its own box made of wood taken from St. John's Kirk in 1894. The mull has all the accoutrements necessary for taking snuff and has engraved silver mountings and other embellishments in the form of one large and two small cairngorms and two large topaz.

The shield-shaped silver plate bears the inscription: "Presented to the Society of High Constables of the City of Perth by Moderator, Office-bearers and Committee of the High Constables of Edinburgh. James Tullo, Moderator, 13 December, 1893." *(See illustration).*

Immediately behind the ram's head are placed the Moderator's Baton and Whistles. The baton is of coromandel wood with silver mountings and was designed and made by David McGregor of Perth. It was gifted to the Society in 1881 by William Burns Thomson who was Moderator from 1880-1882. It is placed on a stand of dark oakwood, the uprights of which are carved in the shape of the city's coat of arms. This is made from a beam taken from the Fair Maid's House and bears the inscription: "Presented by Captain Bannister, Second Division", who held office in 1889.

The first of the Moderator's whistles dates back to the reign of William IV (1830-37) and bears the names of various Moderators from 1850-1877. The other, made of silver mounted ebony wood, bears the inscription: "Presented to the Society of High Constables by Lord Provost McGregor as a memorial of his term as Moderator 1898-1900."

Behind the baton and whistles and ready to the right hand of the Moderator is placed the Ivory Mallet. This and its oak casket were presented to the Society by a few of their guests in 1906. Names include Robert Pullar, John Thomas, John A. Dewar, D. W. J. Nelson, Andrew

Hutchison, W. S. Ferguson, John Begg, John David Sym, F. Norie Miller, Henry Coates, Rufus D. Pullar and A. H. Urquhart.

The Moderator will be wearing the handsome gold chain of office purchased in 1851 and another distinguished piece is the Ex-Moderator's baton of silver-mounted rosewood of the reign of William IV. It was made by R. and R. Keay of Perth and the first name appearing on it is John Henderson, 1880.

Also exhibited at the top table, when held, are the angling, bowling, curling and golf trophies.

Angling has the inscription; "Presented by James Rae King C.A., Moderator of the City of Edinburgh 1926-27 for Annual Competition between the Fishing Clubs associated with the Edinburgh and Perth Societies of High Constables."

Bowling bears the lettering: "The High Constables Bowling Trophy, Presented by the High Constables of Perth to be competed for annually with the High Constables of Edinburgh." This dates back to 1919.

Curling is in the form of a curling stone and carries: "Presented by the Perth Society of High Constables for competition between the Perth and Edinburgh High Constables Curling Clubs - 22nd February 1924."

Golf is inscribed: "Presented by the Members of the Edinburgh High Constables Golf Club to be played for annually between the High Constables of Edinburgh and Perth - 1913."

On the table of each of the six divisions are placed the respective captain's batons.

The First Division Baton was gifted by ex-Lord Provost Kirkwood Hewat in remembrance of his connection with the Society as Captain on the occasion of Queen Victoria's first visit to Perth in 1842. It is made of silver-mounted ebony and was designed and made by David McGregor of Perth.

The Second Division Baton was gifted by Moderator Thomas Jackson in 1890. It is made of silver-mounted ebony and is also thought to have been designed by David McGregor.

The Third, Fourth, Fifth and Sixth Division Batons are all those of the reign of William IV and were presumably procured with the funds of the Society. Each is made of silver-mounted rosewood designed and made by R. and R. Keay of Perth.

It appears that prior to 1882-1890 there were four divisions and that about that time two new divisions were created with the First and Second Division Batons being altered for the use of the new Fifth and Sixth Divisions.

The Secretary's Baton is of pinewood with painted crown surmounted with a silver crown. It carries the inscription: "Used by William Law, High Constable in the reign of George IV. Presented by his grandson, Treasurer Martin - December 1905."

The Treasurer's Baton is made of silver surmounted by a silver crown and is inscribed: "Presented by T. Bannister, Treasurer." No exact date of presentation is known but it could have been gifted around 1885.

Since 1943 the Custodier's Baton has been a George III baton. It is possible that there is in existence somewhere a Custodier's Baton somewhat similar to those of the Treasurer and Secretary.

On 6th December 1976 ex-Moderator Harvey Cruickshank presented a candelabrum which had been donated to the Society by ex-Moderators John Darling, William F. Rodger, T. B. Fergusson, Harvey Cruickshank, Tom S. Caird, James K. Cairncross, Andrew A. Gellatly and Dr. David A.S. Martin. It was to match the candelabrum presented at an earlier date by Mr. A. L. Bushnell.

Each of the officers of the society also wear a badge of office on the right lapel on all ceremonial occasions, to the right of their Society badge. A small baton is carried at the quarterly meetings while the members' own large batons are now only carried on special ceremonial parades. The Moderator's silver chain and whistle was replaced in 1851 by the present gold chain and medal and the two were "weighed in the presence of Mr. Farney and Mr. Rob Martin at 4 oz. 16 pennyweights." The present badge worn by all members was first authorised in 1895.

Finally, the gavel and tray came from timber taken from prehistoric remains found when the General Accident extension was being built in the High Street in 1956. The building is now the District Council headquarters and its foundations were dug down to 22 feet when the remains were discovered.

Perth archaeologist Dr. Margaret Stewart was invited to examine the find and said at the time: "The remains of a wattle hut on a rough timber platform, bedded on the mud of the river, were exposed. There was also a timber upright, some six to eight inches in diameter. In between the line of the collapsed wattle framework, there was an infilling of very black 'occupation earth' filled with the shells of fresh water mussels which had obviously been a staple diet of the inhabitants of the hut."

The timber upright was identified as oak, and General Accident arranged to have it fashioned into a gavel and tray and it was presented to the Society in December 1956. *(See illustration).*

The gavel and tray presented by the General Accident,
carved from prehistoric oak remains found when excavating foundations
for the company's extension in the High Street in 1956.

APPENDIX II

MODERATORS

of the

SOCIETY OF HIGH CONSTABLES

1814-31 – Henry Hepburn	1831-32 – Wm. Marshall
1832-34 – John Graham	1834-37 – James Dewar
1837-38 – James McLeish	1838-40 – Sir David Ross, Kt.
1840-42 – John McFarlane	1842-44 – Joseph Ranson
1844-46 – Sir David Ross, Kt.	1846-48 – William Imrie
1848-50 – David Murie	1850-52 – Wm. M. Farney
1852-54 – Thos. Richardson	1854-56 – Charles Shedden
1856-58 – Robert Martin	1858-60 – Wm. Cameron
1860-62 – James Smeaton	1862-64 – Peter McCurrach
1864-66 – Robert Dow	1866-68 – Chas. C. Stuart
1868-70 – John Young	1870-72 – John McNeill
1872-74 – Robt. Robertson	1874-76 – George Kyd
1876-78 – William Muir	1878-80 – John Henderson
1880-82 – Wm. B. Thomson	1882-84 – James Fenton
1884-86 – James McLeish	1886-87 – James Kaye
1887-88 – Malcolm Stewart	1888-90 – Thomas Jackson
1890-92 – Thomas Love	1892-94 – James P. Whittet
1894-96 – John Masterson	1896-98 – Thomas Forgan
1898-99 – David Macgregor	1899-02 – James McNicoll
1902-04 – Robert Keay	1904-06 – Charles Wood
1906-08 – Robert Shaw	1908-10 – W. W. Fyfe
1910-12 – D. S. Lowson,	1912-14 – Andrew Shaw
1914-17 – Thomas Macpherson	1917-19 – James Robertson
1919-19 – Robert A. Hay	1919-21 – William Munro
1921-22 – Donald A. Stewart	1923-24 – Andrew Miller
1925-26 – W. Erskine Thomson	1927-28 – George N. Gray
1929-30 – Walter Stuart	1930-32 – Thomas Harley
1932-34 – Andrew Anderson	1934-36 – Robert Campbell
1936-38 – J. A. G. Sinclair	1938-43 – Dr. P. O. Moffat
1943-47 – John B. MacDonald	1947-49 – Sir Thomas Hunter, Kt.
1949-51 – John Darling	1951-53 – John Grant
1953-55 – David M. Christie	1955-57 – A. S. Munro
1957-59 – Andrew F. Silver	1959-61 – T. B. Fergusson

1961–63 – William F. Rodger	1963–65 – Harvey Cruickshank
1965–67 – T. S. Caird	1967–69 – James K. Cairncross
1969–71 – John Darling	1971–73 – Andrew A. Gellatly
1973–75 – Dr. David A. S. Martin	1975–77 – J. Morris Wood
1977–79 – Robert S. Martin Bates	1979–81 – Ian R. McKenzie
1981–83 – R. David Hunter	1983–85 – Robert W. Young
1985–87 – G. William Bannerman	1987–89 – James A. McCowan
1989–91 – C. Roger P. Ward	1991– – Donald P. McDonald

APPENDIX III

INSTRUCTIONS and REGULATIONS

for

THE SOCIETY OF HIGH CONSTABLES

OF THE

CITY OF PERTH,

by

THE LORD PROVOST, MAGISTRATES, AND COUNCIL.

1830

At Perth, the 4th day of January, 1830,

The which day, the Honourable the Lord Provost, Magistrates, and Council of the City of Perth being assembled, there was taken under consideration, the propriety of establishing proper Instructions and Regulations for the Society of High Constables, when the following were resolved and enacted; viz.

In the first place - The Council confirmed the designation as, "The Society of High Constables of the City of Perth": – and also hereby enacted and declared, that the period of their service shall continue during the pleasure of the Magistrates for the time.

2dly. The Office-bearers of the High Constables shall consist of a Moderator, a Clerk, a Physician, Chaplain and Solicitor, who shall be elected annually by the majority of votes of the Constables themselves, at a meeting to be held annually for that purpose, on the ... day of ..., at eight o'clock, evening. The Moderator shall be ex-officio President at all Meetings of the High Constables; and in cases of an equality of votes, he shall have a casting in addition to a deliberative vote.

3dly. In order to ensure the punctual attendance of the High Constables, and to preserve order and regularity in all their proceedings at their own Meetings, they shall have power, by a majority of votes, which shall regulate all such matters, to frame such bye-laws and minor regulations as they shall deem suitable, applicable to themselves, and which, when so enacted, shall be binding on every individual member of the High Constables, who shall be bound to adhere thereto, and comply therewith in every respect.

INSTRUCTIONS

1st. In cases of breach of the Peace, or violent threats of immediate mischief, or obstruction of a Constable in the execution of his office, as also in cases of felony which he has seen committed, or has information of, from others who are sure of the fact, every High Constable is authorised and required to seize and apprehend the person or persons so seen or suspected, and immediately thereafter to carry them before a Magistrate of the City, to be dealt with according to law.

2dly. Any citizen presenting a regular written complaint against disorderly or riotous persons, either in the street or in a house, the High Constables may take them into custody, and commit them to the Police Office, until examined by the Magistrates, the Sheriff-depute, or his Substitute, or the officiating Judge in the Police Court, as the case may require; and upon any fray or disorder by day or night, or any other sudden accident that may fall out, either in the street, or in any disorderly house, the High Constables shall take all proper care and measures for separating the parties, and preventing any inconvenience that may happen, and shall seize and apprehend the party or parties guilty.

3dly. If any person or persons liable to be apprehended, as suspected of having committed an atrocious crime, shall take refuge in any house, the High Constable shall follow, in order to seize them; and if the door shall be shut against the High Constable, and access refused, he shall take proper measures to prevent their escape; and he may, after displaying his Baton, and notifying who he is, and the purpose of his coming, and on being refused admission, force his way into the house, even to the breaking open of the door, in order to apprehend the accused; and if they shall fly beyond the bounds of a High Constable's charge, or beyond the jurisdiction of the Magistrates, the High Constable may follow and apprehend them; but no High Constable shall break open doors in pursuit of one who flies after committing a breach of the peace, or minor delinquency. - "Under the description of atrocious crimes seems to be comprehended murder; the inflicting of a dangerous wound; rape; assault with intent to commit a rape; robbery; theft committed by housebreaking, picking locks, or the like, or other aggravated theft; breaking into a house in order to commit murder, theft, or other felony." - Tait's duties of a Constable.

4thly. Every High Constable is hereby directed, when he shall seize and apprehend any person or persons as aforesaid, to secure or detain them in the Police Office, or Police Cells, till they can be conveniently taken before a Magistrate, or before the Sheriff-depute or his Substitute, or the officiating Judge in the Police Court, as the case may require; and to state verbally or in writing to the Magistrate the nature of the crime or offence with which they are charged, and any other information he may possess, including the names of the witnesses, or other means of proof.

5thly. That the High Constables of the City may be the more effectually enabled to execute their office, they are hereby empowered to call for the assistance of the Police Officers and Town Officers and the whole neighbours and inhabitants, who are hereby charged, as they shall be answerable, after the Baton is displayed, to assist them: And the High Constables are hereby directed, with all convenient speed, to inform the Magistrates, or Officiating Judge in the Police Court, or one or other of them, of such of the aforesaid persons as shall refuse or neglect to give their assistance.

6thly. On the first alarm or suspicion of a riot, the High Constables shall assemble, as speedily as possible, (without waiting for a regular notice being sent them) in the Council House, which shall be understood to be the rendezvous on all such occasions, there to receive the necessary instructions from the Magistrates; and the High Constables shall at all times receive and attend to such instructions, in the discharge of their duty, as the Lord Provost or Magistrates may enjoin them.

REGULATIONS REGARDING FIRES

1.Upon occasions of Fire, the Moderator shall call out the High Constables, when it shall be their duty to preserve order, and to protect property; to keep the crowd away from the Engines, and those employed about them; and when necessary do all in their power to provide men for working the Engines.

2.The High Constables shall not assume any management, or give any directions whatsoever, except in preserving order, protecting property, and keeping off the crowd.

The Council approved of the foregoing Instructions and Rules, and appointed them to be observed by the Society of High Constables in the public discharge of their office, and that during the pleasure of the Council; and appoint these Instruction, with this Minute, to be printed, and copies delivered to the different High Constables.

Extracted from the Record of the Town Council by

ALEX. MACKENZIE, Conj. Clk.

APPENDIX IV

REGULATIONS

OF

THE SOCIETY OF HIGH CONSTABLES

OF THE CITY OF PERTH

1991

REGULATIONS

PREAMBLE

WHEREAS following the creation of Perth as a Royal Burgh by William the Lion in 1210 the Lord Provost, Magistrates and Councillors of the City and Royal Burgh of Perth appointed and continued to appoint persons called Constables or High Constables to uphold law and order in the City of Perth; and WHEREAS the High Constables took their instructions directly from the Magistrates until the formation of a regular Police Force from which time the High Constables have played only a ceremonial role at the pleasure of Perth Town Council; and WHEREAS by Minute of Meeting of the Lord Provost, Magistrates and Council of 4th January 1830 the High Constables were given power to frame Regulations to preserve order and regularity in all their proceedings at their own meetings, and that such Regulations were duly framed and have over the years been amended to take account of changing circumstances; and WHEREAS by virtue of the Local Government (Scotland) Act, 1973, the role of the Perth Town Council has been undertaken by Perth and Kinross District Council; and WHEREAS further amendments to the Regulations have been duly approved at an Ordinary Meeting of the Society held on 3rd December, 1990 and ratified by Perth and Kinross District Council on 20th March, 1991. The following Regulations shall apply during the pleasure of Perth and Kinross District Council as from the Third day of June, 1991.

I NAME

The Society shall be called "The Society of High Constables of the City of Perth".

II MEMBERSHIP

1. The Society shall consist of not more than 100 members composed of such gentlemen resident or working in the City of Perth or its immediate vicinity as shall be nominated by the Council of the Society.

2. No person shall be admitted to membership until he shall have sworn the Oath of Allegiance in the form annexed hereto in the presence of the Provost or acting Provost of Perth and Kinross District Council.

3. The members shall be formed into six Divisions. The First, Second, Third, Fourth and Fifth Divisions shall consist of seventeen members each. The Sixth Division shall consist of fifteen members. New members shall be enrolled in the Sixth Division according to the date of their admission.

4. Every new member shall pay such entrance fee as the Society shall from time to time determine.

5. Every member shall pay an annual subscription by 1st December of such sum as shall be fixed at the Annual General Meeting of the Society. Payment of the annual subscription shall entitle each member to attend the Annual Dinner of the Society.

6. Every new member will be supplied with a Society tie and a Society badge (which will be worn on the right lapel on Parades and at the Annual Dinner) and with a large and a small Baton. These Batons are the property of the Society and on a member ceasing to be a member of the Society the Batons must be returned to the Custodier, except as aftermentioned.

7. The official ceremonial dress of the Society shall be Morning Coat Suit comprising black coat, striped trousers, black waistcoat, black top hat, white gloves, Society badge and Society tie. Every member shall equip himself with this official ceremonial dress.

8. A member with twenty five years' continuous membership shall be presented with his large Baton, inscribed with his name, which will become his own property.

9. Any two members may propose a person for membership of the Society by completing and lodging with the Secretary a Proposal Form in terms prescribed by the Council of the Society.

III OFFICE BEARERS AND COUNCIL

1. The Office-Bearers of the Society shall consist of the Moderator, Ex-Moderator, Vice Moderator, the Captain of each of the six Divisions, Secretary, Treasurer, Custodier, Auditor, Chaplain, Physician, Solicitor and Jeweller.

2. The Council for the management of the affairs of the Society shall consist of the Moderator, Ex-Moderator, Vice Moderator, the six Captains, Secretary, Ex-Secretary, Treasurer, Ex-Treasurer, Custodier and Ex-Custodier. Five shall be a quorum at meetings of Council of the Society which shall be held as required by the Moderator.

3. The offices of Ex-Moderator, Ex-Secretary, Ex-Treasurer and Ex-Custodier will auto-matically vest in the retiring Moderator, Secretary, Treasurer and Custodier respectively whom failing for any reason in the last holder of the office who is still a Member of the Society.

4. Office-Bearers will hold office for a period of two years and, with the exception of the Auditor, Chaplain, Physician, Solicitor and Jeweller, will not be eligible for re-election to that office until a further period of two years has elapsed.

IV   ELECTION OF OFFICE-BEARERS

1. The Council of the Society shall make nominations for all posts of Office-Bearers other than the posts of Ex-Moderator and Captains. Any Member also may make nominations for any of the posts of Office-Bearer, other than that of Ex-Moderator and Captains by writing to the Secretary at least four weeks before the June quarterly Meeting stating the post and the nomination and including a statement signed by the nominee that he accepts nomination. All nominations shall be intimated on the Agenda for the June quarterly Meeting. The Society shall elect such Office-Bearers from such nominations at the next Annual General Meeting by a majority of votes of the members present.

2. The Captains of three of the Divisions shall retire each year. At the Annual General Meeting the members of each of the three Divisions whose Captain retires shall elect their new Captain from the members of their Division by a majority of votes of the members present of each respective Division. A Captain who during his term of office moves up to a more senior Division shall complete his term of office as Captain.

3 In the case of a vacancy occurring in any of the offices of the Society an Extra-Ordinary Meeting of the Society may be convened and such vacancy filled or alternatively such vacancy shall be filled at the next Quarterly Meeting. Should the vacancy however occur in the Office of Captain the particular Division concerned shall meet under the direction of the Council and elect a new Captain.

4. Office-Bearers so elected to fill vacancies shall hold office during the remainder of their predecessor's term of office and shall be eligible for re-election.

V   MEETINGS AND PARADES

1. There shall be four ordinary meetings of the Society in each year to be held on the first Monday of March, June, September and December. The meeting held in September will be the Annual General Meeting of the Society. Extra-Ordinary Meetings may be called at any time when required by the Moderator or the Council. Members shall bring their small Batons to all Ordinary and Extra-Ordinary Meetings of the Society.

2. The members of the Society shall Parade at any time when requested to do so by Perth and Kinross District Council. Customarily there are two Parades in each year, one for the Kirking of the Council in May, the other for the Remembrance Day Service in

November. Parades are also customarily requested for official visits by the Monarch and other members of the Royal Family and for Freedom of the District ceremonies when members shall carry large Batons.

3. The Society will hold an Annual Dinner for members and their guests on the second Wednesday of December or on such other date as the Council shall decide.

4. All meetings and Parades and the Annual Dinner of the Society shall be called in writing by the Secretary who shall give at least seven days notice for meetings and Parades and twenty eight days notice for the Annual Dinner.

5. At all meetings and Parades of the Society the roll call will be called by the Secretary whom failing the Ex-Secretary.

6. All members shall attend all meetings and Parades of the Society. If any member is unable to attend any meeting or Parade of the Society he shall intimate an apology for absence to the Secretary prior to the meeting or Parade.

VI FINES

1. Members of the Society, with the exception of members with 25 years continuous service and Clergymen, shall be liable for the following fines:-

    (a) 10p for failing to intimate an apology to the Secretary for any Ordinary or Extra-Ordinary Meeting or any Parade of the Society.

    (b) 5p for attending at any Ordinary or Extra-Ordinary Meeting of the Society without his small Baton, payable at the Meeting.

    (c) 10p for attending any Parade without his large Baton when instructed to carry it, payable at the Parade.

2. Fines incurred by members for failing to intimate an apology for Meetings and Parades shall be collected by the Treasurer with the Annual Subscription.

3. Any member losing his large or small Baton shall pay the Treasurer on demand the value thereof as shall be decided by the Council from time to time.

4. All fines shall be credited to the Funds of the Society.

VII GENERAL

1. The Society shall carry out such ceremonial and other duties as are assigned to the Society by Perth and Kinross District Council, and such other civic, charitable, social activities and outgoings as the Council of the Society shall determine from time to time.

2. The Moderator shall on all occasions have command and direction of the members in the performance of their duties. In the absence of the Moderator his duties shall devolve on the Ex-Moderator, whom failing, the Captain present of the most senior Division.

3. Each Captain shall have the charge and command of his Division subject to the over-ruling control of the Moderator. Each Captain on his election shall receive from the Secretary a complete list of his Division which he shall correct when necessary and he shall at all times be able to report the state of his Division. The Moderator shall have power to select an Ex-Captain to fill the place for the time being of any absent Captain.

4. The Secretary shall prepare Minutes of all Meetings and Parades and conduct the correspondence of the Society.

5. The Treasurer shall receive the subscriptions, fines and other funds of the Society and keep accurate accounts thereof and of his disbursements, which accounts shall be made up as at 31st August and audited annually by the Auditor. The audited accounts shall be submitted to the Annual General Meeting of the Society.

6. The Custodier shall have charge of all the property of the Society and he shall keep a record of the same in a book for the purpose. Office-Bearers shall be invested with the official badge and carry on Parades the official Baton pertaining to their offices.

7. The Chaplain shall advise the Society on matters spiritual, the Physician on matters medical, the Solicitor on matters legal and the Jeweller on matters pertaining to the property of the Society.

8. Sporting Secretaries for Angling, Bowling, Curling and Golf shall arrange such fixtures among members and with Kindred Societies as they shall, with the approval of the Moderator, so decide.

9. If any complaint of insubordination, gross misdemeanour or conduct likely to bring the Society into disrepute is made against any member, the Council will have power, after giving such member an opportunity of being heard, and after such further investigations as the Council may think proper, and if it is of the opinion that said complaint has been substantiated, to report accordingly to the next quarterly meeting of the Society with a recommendation that such member shall cease to be a member of the Society. If such recommendation is adopted by said quarterly meeting the member shall cease immediately to be a member of the Society.

10. If any member is absent from four consecutive meetings or four consecutive Parades of the Society without reasonable excuse, or fails to pay any fine or subscription, the Council of the Society shall have power to terminate his membership.

VIII   ALTERATIONS TO REGULATIONS

1. Any member of the Society may, by written notice to the Secretary at least four weeks before any quarterly meeting, propose alterations to these Regulations. The Secretary shall incorporate the proposal on the agenda for that quarterly meeting. If the proposal

receives a seconder at the meeting it will be voted upon at the next quarterly meeting. In the interval the proposal shall be considered by the Council who shall report their opinion thereon to the next meeting. If the proposal be approved at the said next meeting, with or without amendment, by two thirds of the members present, it shall thereafter be submitted to the Perth and Kinross District Council and, if approved by the said District Council, these Regulations shall be altered accordingly.

2. The Council of the Society may by intimation on the agenda of any quarterly meeting propose alterations to these Regulations, which proposals will be voted on as aforesaid at the following quarterly meeting.

THE OATH OF ALLEGIANCE

I do Swear that I will be Faithful and Bear true Allegiance to Her Majesty Queen Elizabeth, Her Heirs and Successors according to Law, And I further Swear that I will well and truly Serve our Sovereign Lady Queen Elizabeth in the Office of High Constable of the City of Perth and will Loyally and Faithfully perform the duties of that Office and will do Right to all Manner of People after the Laws and Usages of this Realm, without Fear or Favour, Affection or Illwill. So help me GOD.

APPENDIX V

THE OATH OF ALLEGIANCE

High Constables in common with all citizens of Great Britain bear a natural allegiance to their Sovereign. A High Constable holds a quasi-judicial office and in bygone centuries was charged with the duty of maintaining law and order in the locality. It is right and proper therefore that a High Constable must signify this natural allegiance by swearing an Oath of Allegiance to the Sovereign.

The Oath, which is sworn before the Provost of Perth and Kinross District Council, is as follows:-

"I do swear that I will be faithful and bear true allegiance to Her Majesty Queen Elizabeth, her heirs and successors according to law. And I further swear that I will well and truly serve our Sovereign Lady Queen Elizabeth in the office of High Constable of the City of Perth and will loyally and faithfully perform the duties of that office and will do right to all manner of people after the laws and usages of this realm, without fear or favour, affection or ill-will. So help me God."

The taking of an Oath is hallowed by use in the Society but its content has changed over the years. The present Oath is an amalgam of the two Oaths taken by Court of Session Judges, Sheriffs and Justices of the Peace as required by the Promissory Oaths Act of 1868 namely: The Official Oath

"I do swear that I will be faithful and bear true allegiance to Her Majesty Queen Elizabeth her heirs and successors according to law. So help me God."

and The Judicial Oath

"I do swear that I will well and truly serve our Sovereign Lady Queen Elizabeth in the office of ..... and I will do right to all manner of people after the laws and usages of this realm, without fear or favour, affection or ill-will. So help me God."

The swearing of the Oath of Allegiance binds the High Constable not only to observe the motto of the Royal Burgh of Perth "Pro Rege Lege et Grege" ("For the King, the Law and the People")and the motto of Perth and Kinross District Council "Pro Rege et Libertate", (For Law and Liberty") but to observe his original duty to KEEP WATCH and WARD for the Queen.